Ash

Ash

Sharan Strange

Introduction by Sonia Sanchez

Barnard New Women Poets Series

Beacon Press
Boston

Beacon Press
25 Beacon Street
Boston, Massachusetts 02108-2892
www.beacon.org

Beacon Press books
are published under the auspices of
the Unitarian Universalist Association of Congregations.

Printed in the United States of America

05 04 03 02 01 8 7 6 5 4 3 2 1

This book is printed on acid-free paper that meets the uncoated paper ANSI/NISO specifications for permanence as revised in 1992.

Text design by Sara Eisenman
Composition by Wilsted & Taylor Publishing Services

Library of Congress Cataloging-in-Publication Data
Strange, Sharan.
Ash / Sharan Strange ; introduction by Sonia Sanchez.
p. cm.—(Barnard new women poets series)
ISBN 0-8070-6863-2 (pbk.)
I. Title. II. Series.
PS3569.T691229 A9 2001
811'.6—dc21

00-012020

for

my late grandmother, Julia Lucille Clarkson Collie,
my mother, Frances Helen Collie Strange,
and my aunt, Thomasenna Collie Huggins,
all of whom have been my mothers,

and in memory of my father,
James Strange

fire of the venture
ash of the unknown
—**Bei Dao**, *Absence*

contents

Introduction by Sonia Sanchez xi
Acts of Power 1

I. Childhood 5
Zodiac: For Julie 6
How to Teach Them 7
Froggy's Class 11
The Bicycle Wizard 13
Grandmother's Clothes 14
The Crazy Girl 16
Jimmy's First Cigarette 18
Dorothy 19
Barbershop Ritual 20
Mule 22
February 19, 1994 23

II. Snow 27
Outhouses 28
Promise, in a Southern Town 30
Miz Mattie 32
Streetcorner Church 33
Streetcorner Church II 34
Matador 35
Last Supper 36
Words during War 38
The Unintended Life 40
The Widow 41
The Factory 43
Night Work 44
Portraiture 46

III. First Sight 49
Looking 50
Transits 51
Seduction 53
The Apprentice Dreams of Promotion 54
Natural Occurrences 55
Hunger 56
The Stranger 58
Taking a Train 60
The Body 62
Ash 63
Still Life 64
Offering 65

Acknowledgments 67

Introduction

Sonia Sanchez

Octavio Paz said: "When I am writing a poem, it is to make something an object or organism that will be whole and living, something that will be whole and living, something that will have a life independent of me." Sharan Strange's poems do just that. They tell us stories about barbershops and churches. Mothers and grandmothers. This American hunger—physical and psychological. Her words insinuate themselves into our bloodstream, make us want for a moment of truth or illumination. What tempers her poetry? I would say a craft, economical in style, a subtle, lyrical passion, that shimmers even when the self barely survives. These poems resound with soldiering on this battlefield called life. Sharan Strange leads us back to "ash," volcanic in memory, human in their cremation when "even the remains, / sifted," settle over us all.

Ash

Acts of Power

At 8,
the magnets of my fickle thoughts
were three: school, boys, and play.
They freed me from home's cell.
At school, I pleased benevolent wardens
with mathematical and verbal skill.
    Boys
were mine to climb trees with, hunt
blackberries and plums, plot strategy
in simulated war. One boy, my brother,
tirelessly taunted me in games of tag.
He'd let me come *this close* before
springing out of reach. . . .
        Play
went on mostly inside my head. I
devised a life that appeased some inner
god, that plucked a chord in me to sound
I AM, and released me from the stasis
of numb things. It spun me out like a top
dancing to the world's bright limits; then,
responding to a rhythm arbitrary and true,
arced me back to the axis, communal core.
                I sat
in a field among tall green reeds whose
cayenne-colored tips waved like anemones.
We'd suck the salty juices from the stalks.
Taste of our thirsting bodies, taste of
the source of life, the sea.
                        Drunk

on their tears, I ran toward home
and in the road between collided
with the sudden car. Rebellious brakes
halted it—no, I! It sent me hurtling—
a sprung torpedo singing home—
acceded to a force more delicate
and braver than its own.

I.

Oh Sophie, darlin', you say "History" but that means nothing. So many lives, so many destinies, so many tracks go into the making of our unique path. You dare say History, but I say histories, *stories.* The one you take for the master stem of our manioc is but one stem among many others . . .

—**Patrick Chamoiseau**, *Texaco* (translated from French and Creole)

Childhood

Summer brought fireflies in swarms.
They lit our evenings like dreams
we thought we couldn't have.
We caught them in jars, punched
holes, carried them around for days.

Luminous abdomens that when charged
with air turn bright. Imagine!
mere insects carrying such cargo,
magical caravans flickering beneath
low July skies. We chased them, amazed.

The idea! Those tiny bodies
pulsing phosphorescence.
They made reckless traffic,
signaling, neon flashes forever
into the deepening dusk.

They gave us new faith
in the nasty tonics of childhood—
pungent, murky liquids promising
shining eyes, strong teeth, glowing skin—
and we silently vowed to swallow ever after.

What was the secret of light?
We wanted their brilliance—
small fires hovering,
each tiny explosion
the birth of a new world.

Zodiac: For Julie

You set the flame against your hem.
Greedy fingers stole up

your clothes, then your body.
At five, dancing light was

your first fascination. Brother and I
came running, pitched waves rushing

the shore. The little, leaking jars—
our offering wasn't enough

to quench you. You wanted assurances,
like lullabies, or the twinkle of stardust

and moonglow to shower you with wishes.
But you got the sun's arrogant heat,

a blanket threatening to smother you.
A lie hid your shame.

We kept the secret ten years,
a birthmark our shared constellation.

I've long since forgiven you
for the blame I bore. The thundercloud

on my thigh
is your scar too.

How to Teach Them

I. Grooming

Maybe she saw God the Father lurking
behind each seven-year-old's face—
thirty pairs of eyes watching her, judging.

For twenty-odd years the same crop of bad
and good—their mamas, uncles, cousins.
So many ruined. Insolent. Unkempt.

Thirty offspring every year,
she never wanted to push one
out of herself. What world

could they have outside her own?
How to teach them that happiness
would come only from acceptance,

that beauty begins with cleanliness.
Her classroom was as orderly
as her childless home.

II. Beauty

TV pageants had shown us
how to line up, be sorted.

I pitied the boys who had to pick us.
They must've seen those contests too.

What we saw had everything to do
with love, the promise of it.

The screen was a greedy mirror
withholding the goods,

reflecting our hunger. Desire
and denial, at once, our ration.

At school, we learned those adult dramas,
learned that our bodies could betray us.

Our teacher urging each one,
the boys chose eagerly,

shunning the darker girls, their moving
lips, their accusing eyes.

III. Economics

When Mrs. Harris slapped my brother
his nose bled—an instant protest.
It kept up for hours—at school, on the bus,
at home. Neither the silver key hung
down his back on a string nor the wad
of brown paper under his lip could quell it.
We didn't consider charges, a lawsuit,
but accepted the principal's astute
offer: a year of free lunch.

IV. Citizenship

One white teacher in a black school,
young and pretty, her place assured.

We learned about belonging
from a civics assignment:

Find out the origins
of our family names.

My father's answer made perfect
sense to me, though it angered her:

They came from the slave master—
that's how our people got them.

Yours? From a white man called Strange.

Froggy's Class

South Carolina, 1969

She was an old maid, Froggy was,
and she was mean, with bulging eyes
that strained more when she got cross,
and a lumpy sack of gland-swollen throat.
We thought her some crazy crone who
took delight in chastising the innocent.
Her classroom seemed our punishment,
as we were dubbed the smart ones.
But among our bunch the usual stunts
were devised, and her madness was
the antidote to our attempts at anarchy.

I mostly don't remember her abuses—
except the shrill, cracking voice
that harangued us daily, or the hard-rapped
satisfaction of a ruler across knuckles—
but in them she was democratic.
She also favored the word *nigra,*
which made Tina Fogle snicker
and eye me triumphantly. One day reciting
vocabulary, Stuart Williams, brilliant-haired,
the class sweetheart—whose liberal parents
no doubt had drilled its pronunciation—
corrected her, loudly enunciating *nee-gro,*
amid a chorus of halfhearted mimics.
Froggy bristled, glared at his cheerful
nerviness. I loved him for it.

Then after the year-end spelling test, which
I alone aced, she railed against my all-white

peers, summoned me to stand before
the *knuckleheads* she said (or warned)
might someday fall victim to my supervision.
On the last day, silently driving me home,
she pushed a heavy bound notebook
into my hands, and I—out of discomfort
at being alone with her, and shame at
my squalid, small house—scrambled out
of the car, barely caught *will make something
of yourself* and *college* and *proud.*

The Bicycle Wizard

for my grandfather

His yard was a grave for lost wheels and frames,
like the aftermath of some crash derby.
I loved to watch as he tinkered, hoped
in vain for one custom-built, but unclaimed.
He'd lay out parts in schematic array, then
match sprockets and gears, rig and oil chains,
bolt seats, and clean spokes—silent all the while.
Then came the slight smile as he stood each
reincarnation against the barn. Sometimes

he'd let my older brother borrow one,
and for a few hours, I relished the feel
of my hands gripping the wide handlebars
and my small body hoisted above the earth.
I straddled those oversized bikes
wanting to speed, to soar, as he did,
over the smooth road between our houses
where I couldn't go unless on errand, where
I might ride to its end and turn into the world.

But I bumped along in tight circles, spinning
over the rutted, bald ground of my backyard,
missing the pecan and gum ball trees by a hair,
skirting heaps of lumber, rusted motors, pipes,
a shedful of tools—my father's years of junk.
With feet grazing the pedals and crotch
against the crossbar, I kicked and careened
until, throwing myself off, I stopped.

Grandmother's Clothes

The green paisley dress lasted
years past 5th grade. My hair
in neatly braided rows, and the glasses
askew on my nose remind me
of you, doggedly rethreading the Singer,
aligning pieces of cloth with
the care and precision of a physician
resetting bones, sometimes until
dawn, like a herald, roused you.

Homemade yellow Easter and school
pageant outfits, later showing up
at knees, cuffs, as cleaning rags,
swatches in a quilt's design.
Gleaming baptism robes, stark
and clean as I thought your soul must be.
Graduation sleeves that winged me
out into the world, yards of memories
unfolding across your lap.

The year before the polka-dotted
tangerine micro-mini worn to Frankie's
6th birthday—so brief it was transformed
into dust cloth without shredding—I ran
the block to grandparents', your arms
a haven, his shotgun a remedy to
Daddy's anger. He'd stabbed Mama, sliced
red poppies cradling baby sister,
six months in the womb. I didn't stop

to look for blood, gone from my mother's face,
which bobbed and floated, pale and luminous as
the naked kitchen bulb glaring behind
my father's head. I couldn't get near the knife.

Mother and child survived,
so you buried it with your anger.
The dress? Buried too—
or burned—the only one lost it seems.
Some things, you said, I just won't hold on to.

The Crazy Girl

She was given to fits.
So was her brother.
There was a category
for him. *Retarded,* they said.
Something nearer to sin named her.

Oh, the family claimed
its share of deviance—meanness,
generation after generation
of drunks, rootworkers, fools,
feuds carried on with
the extravagant viciousness of kin.

But hers was an unpredictable
violence—more disturbing because
she wasn't a man, besides
being a child. So they settled on
puberty—the mysterious workings
of female hormones—until she
outgrew it and the moniker stuck.

It accounted for the rage
worn on her face, tight as a fist,
fear and restlessness in eyes
like July 4th's slaughtered pig.
Rebellious, woolly hair only
partly tamed by braids, she often
inflicted pain during play.

Boys her favorite victims,
she tore clothes, skin,
marked virgin expanses of face, neck, arms
with scars like filigreed monograms.

Her notoriety was assured when,
at 16, she disappeared, leaving
rumor to satisfy the family's need
to understand, giving context to
her uncle's slow slide into madness,
her sullen body bruised by constant
scratching, as if she could
somehow remove his touch.

Jimmy's First Cigarette

The tobacco sweetness filled your head
with a gentle wooziness, a lightness
that rocked you off-center,
numbing you to the possibility

of pain or cruelty in the world.
From your grandmama's porch
you surveyed a lush green countryside
murmuring with the traffic

of laughing birds, wild animals
and ghosts. You felt alive,
aglow with sensation as,
at her urging, you inhaled

the slim token of freedom.
Pleasure, short-lived, gave way
to confusion, betrayal,
as a torrent of blows

from your daddy's belt broke
your childish reverie—he
and Grandmama conducting
your abrupt trip back to reality.

Dorothy

Being a foster kid gave her second-class
status, but she was still our hero.
An outcast like us, she was an ally against
school bullies and neighborhood brats.
Though we were all poor, she was rejected
for more simple-minded, human reasons.
With smoke-dark skin, hair no longer
than a snap, and legs covered with sores,
any hope she nursed of being found
desirable or cherished was revoked.
She retaliated with a physical prowess
that awed us. Endless chores gave her
muscles to rival the older boys'
and she stunned them in short breathless tussles
that often drew blood. We envied her a body
whose strength matched its rage.
At fourteen, she could beat a man.
In our small world, she seemed invincible,
until we learned her one weakness:
a love for my brother that, unreturned,
provoked the only fight she willingly lost.

Barbershop Ritual

Baby brother couldn't wait.
For him, the rite of passage
began early—before obligatory heists
of candy and comics from neighborhood stores,
before street battles to claim turf,
before he might gain
the title "Man of the House"
before his time.

Each Saturday, he stepped up to the chair,
the closest semblance to a throne
he'd ever know, and laid in for
the cut, the counseling of older dudes,
cappin' players, men-of-words,
Greek chorus to the comic-tragic fanfare
of approaching manhood.

Baby brother's named for two fathers.
He sought them in that neutral zone of
brotherhood, where manliness sprouted
in new growth week by week,
and dark hands deftly shaped identity.

Head-bowed, church-solemn,
he shed hair like motherlove and virginity,
weightier than Air Jordans and designer
sweats—euphemistic battle gear.
He received the tribal standard:
a nappy helmet sporting arrows, lightning

bolts, rows of lines cut in—New World
scarification—or carved logos (Adidas,
Public Enemy) and tags, like hieroglyphic
distress signs to the ancestors:
Remember us, remember our names!

Mule

I sat in the high-backed chair facing your bed,
silence and the long day between us. I listened
for a sound of need from you, grown smaller,
almost lost to the shadows enclosing the room.
I was nine and brave, they said, to do this.

The cancer had attacked your throat and stomach.
I didn't know the pain you felt,
just that you were weak, could eat only liquids
drawn through a tube. How it reduced you
from the tough, angry grandfather who frightened us,
who shouted and cursed his wife,
gold-grey eyes glinting like a blade.

Before illness whittled you all the way down
to pride, you worked full days with a mule
hard-driven through the boss's land. You warned us
never to stand behind it, so I took its twitching,
pointed ears, unblinking eyes, and rooted stance
for stubbornness, disregard, connected this to you.

Only the whistle and tick of your lungs
answered that you were still there, not yet
become spirit under my patient gaze.
You never betrayed what surely was brokenness,
the suffering that consumed you
even before it ruined your body. For months
you held on, until school ended my vigil
and I woke one morning to hear you'd gone.

February 19, 1994

In memory of Julia Lucille Collie

We're all in a black line saying good-bye.
My brother, the oldest grandson, looks lost,
his red face buoyed by whiskey. He holds
our mother, shattered, but dignified,
the way we'd hoped she'd be.
Her black suit and hat are armor.
Tears move down her face like wax.
My aunts, svelte, New Yorkish,
taste a private, refined sorrow.
My sisters cling to each other. They are
on the verge of this world, seeing her gone.
We all are: family, friends, neighbors, church.
The choir wails over their hymnals
as the soloist's strident notes hover. The minister
raises the Bible, chants a prayer to
"send our Sister home." I clutch a book
of poems, turn to the one written for her,
and read, over and over, each word.
Later, I'll sift through the box my mother
drags from beneath the bed, take
the flowered, cotton dress, a safety pin
piercing its pocket. A keepsake
to soften grief,
folded and parceled
like a pillow.

II.

The gestures of the individuals are not history;
but they are the images of history.
—Muriel Rukeyser

Snow

for Toi Derricotte

It came once, the year I turned ten.
That year they told us how we
would become women, and I began
my monthly vigil. But this was
the miracle, singular, unexpected.

The whites had finally stopped
resisting. Unwanted at their school,
we went anyway—*historic,* our parents
intoned, eyes flashing caution
to our measured breaths.

That first martial autumn mellowed
into a winter of grudging acceptance
and private discontent, a season of hope
shaped by fists and threats.
Then angels molted, pelting all

of creation with their cast-off garb.
We went home early, drifting through
a landscape of sudden ghosts,
the yard churning in frothy waves,
as if by an invisible tide of protestors.

What I remember most is its rude
coldness, stinging and wet. How we
mixed it with milk, sugar, vanilla,
into a poor child's ice cream that
melted before we could savor it.

Outhouses

They flanked Southern
country homes like
chimneys, humble stations,
roof slanted like
a tipped hat,
a thing settling
on its haunches.
A skirt of
high grass was
a warning of
unhabitation, human
abandonment, a possible
harborer of snakes.
Building or moving
them was communal,
like a hog
slaughter, and if
we all had
them, a leveler,
like the idiot
sibling, less shameful
than a nuisance,
easy to accept
or overlook.
They were also
ignoble, embarrassing—
a badge of
poverty in town,
the weather-worn

walls, the stench
in summer's heat.
We'd heard of
two-seaters—companionable—
Who had those?—
knew the inconvenience
of items fallen
in—wallets, puppies—
that needed retrieving.

Promise, in a Southern Town

To be a man, was that it?
What they ask of you. . . .
To say I survived hardly matters.
It was real *cracker country,* i.e.,
I was not safe in that town.
My sister Tallie told everyone how
I was a bad boy. But in that place
I wasn't meant to live. I tested
the sheriff at eleven. Barely able
to drive my daddy's truck, I took
him through miles of corn-stubble
and cotton brambles before,
as they say, the jig was up. I'll bet
my parents' moonshine eased his ire,
because I decided when to leave
that town. Then the army—not to be
their version, but out of wanderlust. There,
my drinking habit took hold. How else
to bank the rage? So many ways
to thwart a man. . . .
Family—does that make a man?
To preside over a house? a wife?
To make a wage—and drink it up?
To bury father, brothers, sister,
mother? To do the common work?
To prepare my sons. . . .
Well, I was a man with schemes.
Not to answer to their laws,
not to be bound. . . . I came back

to that town, the factory or shop,
punched out each day and looked down
at *my hands?* that might have killed
at their contempt and disregard.
Instead I walked away—each day,
twenty thousand days, and I died,
not wanting not to live,
nor my name on their lips, undelivered.

Miz Mattie

1.

In the end, rumor thickened to truth.
Everyone said Miz Mattie *worked roots*.
Her food became suspect: noxious
concoctions she brought to the sick
dumped before they got in the house.
Stunning once, she'd wrapped handsome legs
around her men. In the street with a beau,
she'd throw her head back, laughing,
cradling him in the crook of a knee.
Nobody knows when Miz Mattie turned
to that other practice—before the gangrene
set in or after. . . . A lost limb wasn't all
she had in common with Eva Peace.
She was a natural force, admired and feared.

2.

Salt on the threshold, or lye-sprinkled steps—
She did her work in the whitefolks' kitchen.
John the Conqueror, Commanding Pepper—
Had her own reasons to conjure. She knew
Their talk, saw how the children shrank away
Or stared. But she went to church as often
As she wanted, didn't when she didn't,
Harnessed all their negative attention.
Miz Mattie in a light-filled neat frame house,
Candles in late night, in midday, burning—
With her simple husband, son, and daughter,
Charms buried beneath a black walnut tree—
Kept a community at watch and prayer,
She was a natural force, admired and feared!

Streetcorner Church

Is grace delivered
on twilight wings of air?
Don't ask this congregation.
They'd shout *"Yes!"*
then breathe mightily
to draw you in.

A speaker strapped
to a car roof floats
gospel—a curbside choir-in-the-box.
Graffitti-scored stone for pews.
The ceiling dispatches prayer
straight upstairs.
Dubious oasis, Jesus might've shed
bitter tears here.

Three would-be saints
in red-stained garb stroll by,
mockingly sound the refrain:
"Sinner won't you come?"
The sun seeps burgundy,
gone-to-glory behind the altar.
The humming air of deliverance
lingers like a cloying perfume.

Streetcorner Church II

for James Baldwin

The curious parade, stop
to stare as we sway
and shout . . . then hurry on.
A spectacle that turns off nonbelievers.
Or is it the alley's sour, alcoholic breath
that sends them reeling?

We don't know enough shame
to go inside. No, we stand
in plain view, pass the chalice,
a tambourine, like gypsies,
read the spectators, size them up.

The fire in us let loose
could consume this hell-bent world,
this trick floor we believe in.
Instead it rises out of us in song,
mushrooming clouds of faith that
cling to us like debt and sorrow.

I watch you pass—brothers,
sisters, with eyes that look scared,
hard, closed and mysterious
as the heart's dark rooms.
Your anguished faces mirror mine.
I might be among you
if I wasn't fifteen and the preacher's boy.
Their hope and dowry. The one
they intend to save for these streets.

Matador

after the film by Pedro Almodóvar

Large crowds gather
        at public killings
craving justice
        or something
with that warm feel to it.
        The ritual winds
in patterns of figure 8s, turned
        on their side, to symbolize
infinity, eternity.
        The red cape wriggles
like a tongue goading
        a loose tooth. It trembles
like a question, a private joy, a vivid
        host absorbing desire.
Seduction is a dance
        the children already know
and each move here glitters
        like a promise. Anticipation
is a hollow egg
        balanced on a sword tip. How is
the brute to know
        life's made for this?
No matter, matador.
        A thirst for death looms in us all.
Show him red;
        show the bull what's to come.

Last Supper

I've seen hogs herded for slaughter.
Penned on the truck, they whine like saws
biting into reluctant trees. Exiting,
their last exercise is a wild dance
skirting madness, a graceless capitulation.

I witnessed Herman—
who learned his name, ate from my hand—
and his holy-eyed terror said more to me
than any apostle's text. Poor swine,
surrogate Christ, you got no redemption
though you left this world your blood and body.

"You don't eat meat? No wonder you're so thin!"
But will gauntness save me, make me
thin enough to slip the knife, noose,
shackles, or the needle's eye?
Could any of us escape the legacy
of Christ's body offered up to save us,
the legacy of bloodshed that continues
in the name of God and State?

A *Village Voice* reporter tallies
"Final Meals Requested by Inmates
Executed in Texas: Steak was the entree
most frequently asked for . . . seven T-bones
and one smothered. Hamburgers and
cheeseburgers were next at six."

On death row, flesh is the redeemer,
a final consolation. The industry
of slaughter feeding dead men—reluctant
sacrificial calves, marked, their fate
decided nearly from birth. With T-bones
they get the cross, though it's beheaded.
They get the apportioned body,
a sanctioned measure of salvation.

Words during War

January 1991

The landlady's low hum of Spanish
prayer mixes with the sound
of eastbound planes overhead. She
lights candles for the people there
who are under siege, who will get
no food, no water, and cannot,
without the bomb's flash, see
a loved one's face. I glimpse
her family now and then, hear
their cadenced voices, the heavy thumping
of their steps. I'm taunted by
the spicy smell of rice and beans
simmering in her kitchen below me. The walls
chatter, breathe salsa, their heartbeat
insistent as my own. The house
we live in, partitioned, some country
with parts seceded, a body
amputated. Blood, flesh, bone,
skin—warm boundaries holding us—
and words, reducing us always
to language, destiny, intention.

When the rhythms I move to
are disrupted by hourly reports
from the battlefront, I let
the barrage explode around me, grasp
at meanings that linger like artillery's
smoke trails or the dust cloud shadows
of fleeing refugees. Downstairs,

stillness descends like fallout. Outside,
underground darkness, the electric
tremors of people passing.
I feel the gentle thrumming silence
of our house this evening. I think
of those others in the desert, their speech
a code unbroken, their vigilance and
combat breathing, the twisted, glowing wreckage
of their land like a loveless machine.

The Unintended Life

Flowers pulled from her garden
make a space to which they cannot return,
which closes in on itself in healing.
She puts them in water to save them,
to claim them again. They are glorious
in their sharp beauty, already dying.

Her story begins likewise: uprooted
from the sweet soil of her beginnings.
Now it comes in silence—the unintended life—
and again, she relives the night,
his moist breath on her face,
the hot grip on her throat, sheets
staticky and rough like skin peeling off.
She remembers nothing, her mind blank.
No, that scene, like a snapshot—
Still. No sound. A mouth of screams
muffled as if covered by her own hand.

Her body is a vessel of memories sealed tight,

her divided self beckons in mirrors,

the world passing through her. . . .

The Widow

At eighty, the mind locks on some things like a trap.

In her secretest heart she hasn't given him up—a boy who in manhood must have grown more beautiful than when they had been lovers, in youth. A man who had prospered, made many children, and, with only the customary dalliances, honored one wife. Now, in her declining years, the old anger returns and she cannot mourn.

Since her last husband, the boy has become an obsession, filling her dreams, eclipsing memories of both late husbands. They had been good men, kind, and she had found comfort with each, though no passion. But she thinks only of the boy, though with each rankling thought of him, her heart squeezes with resentment.

This boy had been manly—that old cliché—graceful and spirited. He'd indulged his appetite for life, yet was considerate, compassionate, intellectual. Perfect in form, he had respected and nurtured his body. What a sensualist he'd been, but with such sensitivity and proper discrimination! She wonders if the man who had been that boy still has such qualities, and if he is still alive. He had written to her some years afterward apologizing, it seemed, that life's vicissitudes had kept them apart, and that he had married but would always cherish . . .

How false their pleasure had been!—like a mistaken prize reclaimed by another. How exacting and faithless love was, how impartial in its going. . . .

She curses this wound of old hurt, betrayal of the past revisited. Each reminder of her loss floods the synapses with disappointment and a new pattern of discontent hums in her. Her thoughts are bewildered, bitter. She despises those who sing so sweetly, so shrilly of facile love. She dismisses any god that would bid her be happy, especially now when so little matters.

She will go on this way for a while yet. She will go on each day cursing fate, which robbed her of true joy, defying the solace of faith or death, her heart renewed by anger, that boy—against all belief—keeping her alive.

The Factory

Talking about silkscreening, my aunt remembers her first job in New York, decades ago, at the Sample Co. near Chambers St., where she pressed glue through screens and stuck fabric pieces to boards. She was 18, scrawny, and no one's idea of an employee. In the employment office week after week, she met an ugly girl who made her laugh, and so went home with her. The city was full of people, and forgetting caution, she'd go wherever invited back then, even out to Brooklyn or to Queens. The factory was its own community, a motley group of natives and new arrivals, desperate or hopeful. Married or not, everyone, it seemed, found a lover there. But those who lacked the efficacy of English toiled all day, mute as machines. *What became of them?* Some escaped her. Others, who were long since hidden, come forward now, pushed by memory's levers. All left an imprint. *The German immigrants, I'll never forget them:* Casamia, the gypsy, and "Crazy Judy," nervous, saluting the boss with their number tattoos. Gentle Herman, jumping to his feet, clicking his heels.

Night Work

In the changeling air before morning
they are silhouettes. Dark ones
with the duskiness of predawn on them
and the shading of dust and sweat.
Busying themselves in buildings,
on scaffolds, and on the black
washed pavements, they are phantoms
of the city—guardians of parking lots
and lobby desks, tollbooths, meters,
the all-nights and delivery trucks.
At bus stops they are sentinels
and the drivers. Launderers and cleaners
readying the offices and the untidy houses
of privilege. Cooks heaping up meals
for the well fed, the disabled, or the indifferent.
Trash-takers, making room for more.
Nurses, eternally watching.

When my mother, starting the stove
at 5 a.m., looked out the window, she saw
her father, days after his funeral.
Had he come back to the field
and the plowing left undone when
the chain snapped and struck him,
knotting his throat into pain
and its aftershock of silence?
Did he return to reclaim the work
like a part of himself unfulfilled
and his story untold?

He is with us still, she said
to the inchoate brightness.
He is there even now.

Spirits are much the same in those
uncensored hours—flitting dim figures,
half-remembered apparitions, whose industry
renews and undergirds our own.
They are our counterparts: the whispering
echo of that other turning
as we turn in bed, the sigh that heaves
in the wake of some unseen act. In the darkness,
where a cycle of making and unmaking unfolds.
If anything could help us believe in
their benign presence, it is the workers,
perpetual as stars, a collective
of eyes and hands, conjuring.

Portraiture

for my parents

How a woman angled against a fence
becomes a sign. A woman in 1955,
just so, inscrutable eyes.
(She, the escapee of one man's fear,
his year of weeping.) Greeting
the world halfway with serious gaze,
crisp white sleeveless blouse, full
skirt, dime-store lipstick, curls.
And a man coming into her orbit fixes there.

A man, lost and sun-drunk like one
out of her haunted past, beckoning,
respectful, a sign—of what,
redemption? That green uniform
(he never quite escaped its shape)
eclipses the sky, the path,
the distance she must travel
to return home. His eyes are bright,
sly, a little kind. They are young, still
open, yet the intimation of all
that was and is to come flares in that meeting.

Convergence: woman, fence, gaze,
man—a scene as transport. A moment
as bubble in the wind of absolution.
There is no absolute, he thinks,
yet there she is, creator, indifferent almost,
poised to join will to cause,
and he, the seeker
who lays down his things,
who follows her.

III.

I am very hungry. I am incomplete.
And none can tell when I may dine again.
—Gwendolyn Brooks

First Sight

A beginning and like a newborn
you're dazzled by sight. After fifty years
a corridor is no longer a corridor,
a window is solid, holds a picture
like a movie screen. The doctors
have undone a lifetime of darkness—
for what? You still close your eyes,
won't turn on lamps at home.

The city seems a mirage, dishonest
with constant movement, or so shy
it flattens into image, then shimmers.
Seeing is strange! Free of the dark,
sharp spots of color float, shapes wave,
bounce—an endless cacophony of surfaces.
You're vulnerable, trying to fashion it all
into a tapestry that means *this I know.*

This knowledge is surrender, faith.
You've yet to learn you cannot hold
these shapes in your hands, like objects
that marry this world to you. Eyes closed,
all things are yours, in three or more
dimensions. Open, they seem flirtatious
as stars—winking, distant, beyond
touch, receding with the light.

Looking

> I apply myself to "seeing" the world nude, that is,
> almost to e-nu-merating the world, with the naked
> obstinate, defenceless eye of my near sightedness.
> And while looking very very closely, I copy.
> **—Hélène Cixous**

When he wrote the word,
the o's were joined
like eyeglass lenses without
a bridge. Cross-eyed, hypnotic,
they threatened to merge,
become Cyclopean. Myopic,

I copied them.
The chalkboard glimmered miles
away, undecipherable, a blur.
Somehow the boy next to me
could conjure its contents
in dutifully shaped squiggles and lines.

In precise imitation, I repeated, made
his eyes my own, sought windows
into penmanship and spelling. On his page
those jumbled, swimming white letters
were transformed into black ones
that sat apart, still enough to see.

And the o's, those Siamese twins
anchored by consonants on both sides,
seemed to compose the most perfect sign—
round, open, unending, unfolding
to mirror itself, the way sight
offers its version of the world.

Transits

1.

Once Father raised
a broom to me—before
possibility moved in me
like blood, wouldn't flow, just
backed up
on itself, a sluggish creek—
and raised a purple welt
across my cheek.

2.

It didn't happen
on my 14th birthday
like Mama thought,
but a month before
during Sunday service. I stumbled
down, down
to the tiny basement toilet, as
a red-orange map defined itself
on my underwear. Is that how God
claimed Mary? Did she first bleed
in His house?

3.

At this age
or before,
I am henceforth liable

for my sins.
His left hand
covering my heart,
the minister slapped
his right palm hard
against my forehead,
set off flares and blood
erupting. Through vertigo
talk of cleansing.

4.

My husband gone
a year—child too—this
scar reminds me.
Each month I still bleed,
feel the centrifugal
pull, refuse
my Father's house.

Seduction

Not the round, shining globe
of the eye in profile,
nor the fissure of a smile calling,
as the earthquake does, some part of itself
back into itself, nor the curving
spine, an archipelago of promise—
those aspects offer the primal gift.

But voluptuous thoughts, entrusted to words,
and words, the language of careful stones
circling about you,
and the fires those stones make,
the air they eat up all around, leaving
you breathless, the light
they cast reshaping everything,
and the new blood rising
in you, molten, disaster.

The Apprentice Dreams of Promotion

I want to escape sin.
Truth be told, I've done
my share to fight it.
But administrative tasks
dirty my hands, devil's
work I'm left to do. See,

creation is my only desire;
I don't care to bargain
with the natural order. Here,
the chastity of silence would
grant me respite. Obedience
calms the storm in my head.

High above everything,
faces are neutral as slate.
Bodies struggle, sequestered
ants wedded to instinct. I stare
through sparkling glass, marvel how
pain's firebath yields purity, reflection,

how brain-grey stone renders monuments
and skyscrapers. At the summit,
even the air is absolved.
Families of crows with cloud-stuffed
mouths remove the gauzy wrapping
from the healing sky.

Natural Occurrences

Once I pried open my doll's head
seeking a nest of silken hair inside.
But there was none. No inner parts, no
tongue. Just the stubble of glued blond
tufts behind sky-colored, dumb, unrooted eyes.
Odd to find it hollow,
like a fallow garden or a river's empty bed.

I thought I'd find some answer
to the mystery of my own hair,
not smooth or flowing like a doll's
but kinked, knotted, painful to be combed.
Tender-headed, my grandmother called me
as she tugged the stubborn tangles and I cried
until she warned my heart would burst.

She'd say I was *full of woe,* which,
sounding religious, pleased and scared me—
the way I'd felt beheading that doll.
But it was a dead thing that, despite
my tortures, couldn't cry, or understand
the world as I would someday, or why
its falseness made me angry and sad,
and why tears were good.

Hunger

1.

Combing the papers for summer jobs,
nothing that seems absurd now, or
the obvious hustle, was beneath us;
our need was rampant as newsprint,
those endless columns of pulp dreams.
Not old enough for hire, I fantasized
my fortune in stuffing envelopes.
Seductive ads beckoned: *Make $$$!*
No experience needed! (Just gut-
wrenching desire for anything more . . .)
I'd make thousands, save the family,
buy my way out of loneliness,
invisibility. I sent off letters,
stamps tasting of promise,
expectation swelling in me like a secret.

2.

I yearned for glimpses of freedom
like clearings stumbled upon,
meadows of unbroken green
edged by trees, yet seemingly endless.
Like that, but interior, as in the mind's
infinite reaches, hinted at in dreams,
or the openness the heart allows each time
we choose love. Going into fields where
my grandmother eked out a sharecropper's wage,
before I learned they weren't hers,
they too seemed unbounded by horizon.

3.

What I wanted I couldn't name,
but the longing felt more real than
what I could touch, constant as labor.
Some nights I lay on the ground for hours,
drunk with that view of the heavens,
as if those thousand thousand stars each
held me by a thread, their imperceptible shuffle
spinning around me some cosmic cocoon.
So I endured the days, and months,
and years that kept me from adulthood,
the time of fulfillment. Or so I thought.
Growing up brought an end
only to a kind of indentured servitude,
taught me to distinguish loss from lack.

4.

These days it's TV commercials—
the happy clan hawking cars and
fortified cereals—a kind of contentment
bartered for with longing or need.
Anything is attainable in fantasy.
It takes so much to learn just this:
The things we need we don't get in this world.
Some say we're lucky to be alive, to have
our chance each day, to fight, get by. I say
what's luck, or chance, or choice for that matter?
I take the offerings of this slim life,
hunger, like memory, some kind of assurance,
the body, open, unable to be filled.

The Stranger

The one I like most is about her—a story with so few details it became mystery, with so few versions it remains myth. This much I can tell you. She was married, had a family. I know this because her granddaughter-in-law told the story to her daughter, who told it to me. What was she like? I picture her small and lean, brown as pines, with hair like bare branches in winter. Did she grow very old? How did she die? None of this I know, only that she was a dark woman from South Carolina. And she was unpredictable.

She'd come and go as the spirit moved her, disappearing for days without a word. It wasn't a lover who lured her, or a craving for adventure—that was common as dirt yards in those parts. No, it was a calling, a witnessing she had to do. . . . Eventually, not even her husband dared question her. Like the others, he simply waited for her return, waited to see if she had changed. But she didn't appear changed. Only something slight, dimly perceived, hovered about her, like the first glimmerings of new light after the passing of a storm.

Nothing more could be said about her—yes, she could heal them with her roots and leaves. And she could read their dreams. After a time, they grew used to her wanderings. But who wouldn't be intrigued when she came home after a week in the woods, barefoot, with a bag of live snakes, a pale mark blooming on her forehead, and some strange landscape hinted at in her eyes?

That is the truth as it was passed on to me. Did it happen? Who can say. I ponder this sliver of a tale, and her ways, which seem to me those of a wisewoman or shaman. Then there is the real story, the one no one can tell me: what happened in those woods. Half-a-life and no-name, she has been given to me. I come back to her often, gazing in the mirror at a face with its own wild luminance, its own secrets.

Taking a Train

1. Views

Leaving the city, its parks
and circles of benches, its
smokestacks churning chemical
clouds into hazy sunlit sky.

The flash of a tractor trailer cab
on a bridge among a parade of cars—
the shine of commerce, of promise.

Rivers glint silver. It feels like prosperity—
traveling. *Prosperity, possibility*
jingle in my mind like change in a pocket.

Then woods where slender pines huddle,
adolescents awaiting reprieve.
Winter is ending, yet they look
desolate, still mired in snow.

The land breaks into puddles,
ponds like melting tallow. A clump
of overturned tree, black roots
and soil peeled back like a scab.

2. The Route

On countless trips I've counted
the thirty or so reds of fall

in Connecticut's forests, the line
extending to Maine and beyond.

I've glimpsed enclaves of beach
and cottages in Thoreau's wilderness.

Grimy rooftops and chimneys,
warehouses, steeples, back

streets and gloomy stations.
Rush of scenery, blur of recognition.

This train shuttles me between
two cities: Boston's squares and

stolid houses, Brooklyn's brownstones
and vendored streets, each with a river

to comfort me. Transience—
no, displacement, sparks

the hunger to create.
Moving, thwarting stasis, I

transcend mere body, assume
an abiding self. This train

ferries me from two fixed points.
What lies between shimmers, shifts—

a panoramic backdrop I detach from
like a guided tour of some other life.

The Body

Nothing is certain but the body.
—W. H. Auden

The man who is dying of AIDS calls it
a sensual experience—dying—feeling his body
as a newness. The throbbing in his leg
is the beat of his heart. And the shallow breathing.
His body slowly gives itself over to death,
like easing into sleep or a full warm bath.
Only sex has ever made him sense his corporeal self,
now this. But it knows, he says, how to die.
The body tells us when it's time.

After her lover died the poet wrote, "But of course,
there is that business of 'going on living'—
one does it, almost unconsciously—something
in the cells, I think." *In the cells . . .*
and I am reminded that even the smallest
parts of the body are wombs.

When I look at you and speak,
my body asserts itself as consciousness, an algebra
of organs, fluids, enzymes. When I look at you,
and speak—motion of eyes, tongue
a riot in the mouth—I sense myself
beyond other notions of self: history, your
experience of me. I am the interval
between the first quickening
and the last.

Ash

Today sun warms the snow.
It melts and comes apart,
running off in streams,
crosshatching its way downhill.
Water has a destination always—
home, to all other water.
Standing in its path, I'm closed,
a knot of grief, a stone.

I'm remembering your words:
I didn't choose this, and,
Now survive. I hoard my losses
against the chance that more
will be taken from me.
I want what babies want,
sustenance when I call out.
I want belief to seep in
and find its level in me.

I long for the things I destroyed—
our home, this season's food, small
niches that might have been havens—
ground I thought I'd clear by burning—
even the remains,
sifted, and settling over me.

Still Life

What endures? Not the arranged
fruit—Cézanne's apples and pears
long since ruined—but the image.
We hold on to what the light gives us.
As when, in a shining moment
I recall my mother's beauty. I see her
tall, bright, a goddess in my first year
of school, when I felt my smallness,
the smallness of a child. That day
I looked out the classroom window
to the lawn where a woman stood,
brought to life by the sun.
I was proud of her,
because at home she lost that beauty.
At home, she was tired, always
worried, and seemed to smile
only when father wasn't around.
When his insults and threats hit her,
she crumpled and was plain.
But here, she is radiant, aglow
with the red lipstick she loved,
a living sculpture
claiming me as daughter.

Offering

In the dream, I am burning the rice.
I am cooking for God. I will clean
the house to please Him. So I wash the dishes,
and it begins to burn. It is for luck.
Like rice pelting newlyweds,
raining down, it is another veil,
or an offering that suggests
her first duty: to feed him.

Burning, it turns brown, the color
of my father, whom I never pleased.
Too late, I stand at his bed, calling.
He is swathed in twisted sheets,
a heavy mummy that will not
eat or cry. Will he sleep when
a tall stranger comes to murder me?
Will I die this fourth time, or the next?

When I run it is as if underwater,
slow, sluggish as the swollen grains
rising out of the briny broth to fill the pot,
evicting the steam in low shrieks
like God's breath sucked back in.
Before I slip the black husk of sleep,
I complete the task. The rice chars,
crumbles to dust, to mix with
the salty water, to begin again.

Acknowledgments

Thanks to Amy Caldwell and Beacon Press, Barnard College, and Sonia Sanchez.

I also wish to thank the editors of the following journals and anthologies in which many of these poems have appeared, some in slightly different versions: *Agni, The American Poetry Review, Callaloo, The Harvard Advocate, The Radcliffe Quarterly, The Best American Poetry 1994, Bittersweet: Contemporary Black Women's Poetry, In Search of Color Everywhere, In the Tradition: An Anthology of Young Black Writers, On the Verge: Emerging Poets and Artists,* and *The Garden Thrives: Twentieth-Century African-American Poetry.*

I am indebted to the MacDowell Colony, the Corporation of Yaddo, the Gell Writers' Center, the D.C. Commission for the Arts and Humanities, and the National Endowment for the Arts, for support during the writing of many of these poems.

Special thanks to: The Dark Room Collective for making a way out of no way—Thomas Sayers Ellis, especially, for his activism, support, and friendship; the extraordinary Charles H. Rowell; Eric Gudas, for support and thoughtful comments on the manuscript; and Helen Elaine Lee, for providing a place to write and helping me to be heard.

Thanks and respect to friends, fellow artists, and others who've given or furthered my journey: Andrew Adlam, Elizabeth Alexander, Jody Armour, Francisco Baldwin-Tejeda, Vera Beatty, Sasha Berman, DeSharn Boone, Mackie Burnett, Django Carranza, Aya de León, Marjorie Edmonds-Lloyd, Pamela Epps, Percival Everett, Ellen Gallagher, Takako Lanier Giraud, Martin Glynn, Felecia Green, Ricardo Guthrie, Kendra Hamilton, Michelle Banks Herrera, Kerrick Johnson, Blondel Joseph, Jamaki Knight and Survival Soundz, Minkah Makalani, Galen Malicoat, Suzanne McFeeters (we miss you!), Tracye McQuirter, Ailish Meisner, Patricia Mendoza, Opal Moore, Reginald Moseley, Christopher Myers, Kambui Olujimi, Willie Perdomo, Alan Shaw, Michael Veal, Franke Vogl, Aaron Walker, Noland Walker, Timothy Wilkins, Akhaji Worrell, the sister-women of Brooklyn's *Zawadi.*

To Mrs. Mary Kerr and Mrs. Vestina Young, teachers who believed in me; fellow poets, teachers, and staff in the writing program at Sarah Lawrence, especially Thomas Lux, Suzanne Gardinier, Golden Brooks, Dorothy Johnson Laird, Martie Palar, Jane Hodges, Janet Kaplan, Susan Guma; Dr. Joanne V. Gabbin, for the Furious Flower Conference.

And, not least, thanks and love to my family tree (all the branches), but especially to Roz, Jimmy, Julie, Bill, Cynthia, Joyce, Nekee, Aunt Dot, Roland aka MC Huggs, Jeff, and the new generation—Danielle, Jonathan, Jessica—and to the many artists, activists, and thinkers who nurture and sustain me.

To the Creator, and the Ancestors!